The Daily Plan Book for Preschool

Name _____

School _____

Address _____

Phone _____

Cellphone _____

E-Mail _____

School Year _____

Administrator _____

Table of Contents

☆ How to Use This Plan Book

This comprehensive plan book will provide you a means by which to do your best teaching! By simply planning ahead and outlining your basic daily procedures using activity/interest centers, you and the children's day will be much more productive. As the teacher, you will find that you will save both time and effort in a more relaxed classroom atmosphere.

Once your planning has been recorded, this book can serve as a basis for planning next year's activities. Substitute teachers will find that the advance planning you make in this book will provide them a way to assist you in supporting your classroom goals and keeping the children on task. Your step-by-step lesson planning can also be easily checked by your supervisor or director.

DAILY SCHEDULE – Record your general classroom schedule (Monday through Friday) for a quick look at what the children (and you) should be doing throughout the day.

CHILDREN'S INFORMATION – Fill in the information once your permanent classroom list is established. Use pencil in order to allow changes in addresses, phone numbers and/or to add a new child's name. (In case of an emergency, make sure you record parents' cellular phone numbers in addition to home and work numbers.)

SUBSTITUTE TEACHER INFORMATION – Use these pages to inform any substitute teacher of the pertinent information needed to successfully manage your class in your absence. Update this information periodically throughout the year. You may want to reproduce these pages and give them to your supervisor/director.

INCENTIVE PROGRAM AND DISCIPLINE PROCEDURES – Describe the specific procedures you have planned for both rewarding and disciplining the children. Let substitute teachers know what steps you wish them to take before referring a child to the office.

EMERGENCY PROCEDURES – Record your school's procedures for such emergencies as fire, tornado, and earthquake. These procedures should provide any adult in your classroom the information they need to safely evacuate and care for the children. A list of simple health and emergency first aid procedures are noted as a reminder.

CLASSROOM LAYOUT – Pencil in your general play areas and activity/interest centers. The layout will be determined by the size and shape of your classroom and your individualized teaching style. Make sure you plan for traffic areas and clean-up areas.

CHILDREN'S BIRTHDAYS – Write the names and birth dates of the children in the appropriate monthly areas. (You may wish to reproduce the birthday list and post it near your classroom calendar.)

SPECIAL EVENTS – Note your plans for upcoming special events, parties, and field trips. An area to list names and phone numbers of classroom volunteers is also provided.

TOYS SUITABLE FOR PRESCHOOLERS – This specific list notes the toys, equipment and materials appropriate for two, three, four, and five year olds.

MOST PRESCHOOLERS CAN . . . – Young children need new and challenging experiences through fun, playful activities. This list helps you determine what most two, three, four, and five year olds can successfully accomplish.

A Sample **DAILY LESSON PLAN** and a **WEEKLY ACTIVITY/INTEREST CENTERS** Form, using the theme of "Bears," are shown on pages 14 and 15.

DAILY LESSON PLANS – In this plan book you will find enough pages for 52 weeks of lessons. Each lesson plan page has been divided for you to record each day's activities, Monday through Friday. Record your plans for group songs, stories, circle time, special events, outdoor activities, lunch, snacks, and nap time. Keep the plan book open on your desk and refer to it often throughout the day.

WEEKLY ACTIVITY/INTEREST CENTERS – Use these helpful forms to record your weekly plans and seasonal changes for your activity/interest centers. The form lists 12 different centers. No classroom can successfully operate all 12 centers at one time. Use the form to record only those centers you wish to use with your children. Rotate and implement as many activity/interest centers as possible throughout the year.

☆ Daily Schedule

EARLY MORNING SCHEDULE

7:00 – 7:30   _____

7:30 – 8:00   _____

8:00 – 8:30   _____

8:30 – 9:00   _____

FULL-DAY PROGRAM SCHEDULE

8:00 – 8:30   _____

8:30 – 9:00   _____

9:00 – 9:30   _____

9:30 – 10:00   _____

10:00 – 10:30   _____

10:30 – 11:00   _____

11:00 – 11:30   _____

11:30 – 12:00   _____

12:00 – 12:30   _____

12:30 – 1:00   _____

FULL-DAY PROGRAM SCHEDULE (CONT.)

1:00 – 1:30   _____

1:30 – 2:00   _____

2:00 – 2:30   _____

2:30 – 3:00   _____

3:00 – 3:30   _____

3:30 – 4:00   _____

4:00 – 4:30   _____

4:30 – 5:00   _____

LATE DAY SCHEDULE

3:00 – 3:30   _____

3:30 – 4:00   _____

4:00 – 4:30   _____

4:30 – 5:00   _____

5:00 – 5:30   _____

5:30 – 6:00   _____

6:00 – 6:30   _____

☆ Children's Information

STUDENT	DAY ATTENDING					PARENT/GUARDIAN	PHONE HOME WORK	ADDRESS	EMERGENCY CONTACT
	M	T	W	TH	F				

4

⭐ Children's Information

STUDENT	DAY ATTENDING					PARENT/GUARDIAN	PHONE HOME WORK	ADDRESS	EMERGENCY CONTACT
	M	T	W	TH	F				

5

⭐ Substitute Teacher Information

Arrival _____

_____

_____

Snacks _____

_____

_____

Lunch _____

_____

_____

Restrooms _____

_____

_____

Rest Time _____

_____

_____

Clean-Up _____

_____

_____

Story Time _____

_____

_____

Interest Areas _____

_____

_____

Circle Time _____

_____

_____

Dismissal _____

_____

_____

# Children With Special Needs

Name	Comments

Emergency Procedures

Fire Drill _____

_____

_____

_____

_____

_____

_____

_____

_____

_____

First Aid Kit Location _____

_____

_____

People Trained in CPR

_____ Room _____

_____ Room _____

_____ Room _____

Weather _____

_____

_____

_____

_____

Security _____

_____

_____

_____

_____

Health/Safety Precautions
• Record all students' medical problems, allergies and medications.
• Maintain a classroom first aid kit and inform students where it can be found.
• Instruct students about what to do if they feel ill.
• Demonstrate to students how to cover their mouths when coughing or sneezing.
• Have students practice routine hand washing.

Emergency First Aid
• Send someone else to notify the office and to call for an ambulance.
• Do not move a person that is seriously injured.
  Bleeding – Apply pressure directly to the wound. Elevate the wound higher than the victim's head if possible.
  Choking – Stand behind the victim and give abdominal thrusts under the rib cage until the object is expelled (Heimlich maneuver).
  Shock – Place the victim on his or her back with the legs slightly raised. Keep the victim warm by wrapping him or her in blankets.
  Not Breathing – Give mouth-to-mouth resuscitation or CPR (cardiopulmonary resuscitation). To give mouth-to-mouth, clear any object from the mouth. Pinch the victim's nose and cover the mouth tightly with your own. Blow hard enough to make the chest rise. Remove your mouth and release the nose to allow the victim to breathe out. Repeat the procedure every five seconds.
  Note: Adequate training is necessary to successfully perform CPR.

⭐ Classroom Layout

Suggested Guidelines

- Separate quiet areas from noisy areas.

- Define areas by using furniture or shelving.

- Place activity/interest centers near needed resources.

- Make sure you can view all of your room easily.

- Store materials at a height for children's access.

- Keep in mind children's traffic patterns when moving from one center to the other.

- Make sure that the teacher's supplies and materials are kept in a separate department and/or out of the reach of children.

⭐ Children's Birthdays

January

February

March

April

May

June

July

August

September

October

November

December

⭐ Special Events, Parties, Programs, and Field Trips

_____ _____

_____ _____

_____ _____

_____ _____

_____ _____

_____ _____

_____ _____

_____ _____

_____ _____

_____ _____

Rainy Day Procedures

_____ _____

_____ _____

⭐ Materials & Toys Suitable for Most Preschoolers

Remember that equipment and/or materials suitable for a four or five year old are not necessarily suitable for a two or three year old. Please keep in mind that a child should be supervised by a competent adult at all times. Keep small objects that could be swallowed or cause choking away from small children. Make sure that all equipment is in good repair and that all materials and toys are child-safe and non-toxic. Refer to the manufacturer's directions and warnings on all equipment and materials that you use with your children.

TWO YEAR OLDS

Animals, stuffed or plastic

Balls, large rubber or foam

Blocks, large (hollow cardboard or plastic)

Blocks, linking (Legos©)

Boards for building, carrying, walking up inclines

Books, heavy duty and/or cloth

Brushes for painting with water

Bubble blowers

Cardboard boxes, large and sturdy

Child size car (moves by pushing feet or pedals)

Clay, salt clay, Play-Doh© (non-toxic)

Cleaning equipment: broom, mop, dustpan, carpet sweeper

Climbing apparatus with safe, easily accessible platforms

Crayons, large size

Dishes and cooking utensils (unbreakable)

Dolls, doll bed, stroller and clothing

Dress up box: hats, gloves, scarves, shoes, jewelry

Easel and large paper

Hand puppets

Jack-in-the-box

Kitchen toy appliances (child-size sink, refrigerator, stove)

Musical instruments: drum, gong, xylophone, bells

Nesting boxes or cans

Paint, powder paint mixed with water (non-toxic)

Pets: fish, rabbits, turtles, guinea pigs

Rope and string

Sand box and sand toys (scoop, pail, big spoons, sifter)

Slide (small, attached to climbing apparatus)

Suitcase, bags

Table and chairs (child size)

Tricycle

Toys: cars, planes, trucks, boats, trains, dump truck, telephone, ironing board

Wagon

Wheelbarrow

Wooden beads, large with heavy string w/metal tips

THREE YEAR OLDS

Balls, various sizes

Beanbags

Blocks, smaller for building

Boards for balancing, sliding, seesaw, bouncing

Books, picture/story

Building tools (child-size hammer, large nails, soft wood)

Climbing apparatus, jungle gym, boxes, slides, etc.

Color manipulatives

Colored paper

Felt pens (water-based, non-toxic)

Floor puzzles, large size

Fingerpaints

Materials for playing house and store

Musical instruments: tambourine, castanets, triangle

Poster paint in bright colors (non-toxic)

Rocking horse

Scissors, blunt

Sewing cards

Shape manipulatives

FOUR YEAR OLDS

Board games, simple

Bicycle with training wheels

Camera (toy)

Coloring books and art paper

Cooking equipment (toy pots and pans, play food)

Construction toys (fit together type)

Crayons (more colors)

Doctor and/or nurse kit

Dollhouse

Flannel and felt board visuals

Flashlight

Garden tools, small

Jigsaw puzzles

Magnets

Miniature people, animals, vehicles, food

Paste, paper, and materials (beans, macaroni, etc.)

Playhouse and/or tents

Ring toss game

Screwing or twisting toys

Seesaw

Toy sailboat (things that float)

Water play materials

Workbench and small tools

FIVE YEAR OLDS

Card games, simple

Clay (modeling; type that can be baked or fired)

Crafts, simple sewing, loop looms

Dollhouses with miniature people and furniture

Dolls with accessories

Dress up costumes: doctor, astronaut, carpenter, fireman, etc.

Jump/skipping rope

Kites/pinwheels

Play setting toys (farms, stores, gas stations)

Scrapbook (and things to paste in it)

Science materials (magnifying glass, stethoscope, bug catcher jar/net)

Scooter

Toy action heroes or soldiers

☆ Most Preschoolers Can . . .

Young children need new and challenging experiences through fun, playful activities. It is important to know that most preschoolers can do the following activities; however each child matures at his/her own rate and time.

MOST TWO YEAR OLDS CAN . . .

Climb up stairs two at a time

Walk on tiptoes for a short time

March in time to music

Imitate gross motor skills (hands over head, touch toes, clap hands, etc.)

Jump off low step, step over low obstacles

Kick a ball and catch a large ball

Enjoy mud and water play

Put together large puzzle pieces

Name simple pictures in a book

String very large beads

Unscrew the lids of jars

Use a cookie cutter with clay

Enjoy pushing and pulling things

Begin to use pounding and interlocking toys

Begin some painting and coloring

Play with clay and/or fingerpaint

Color with large crayons on plain paper

Begin to tear paper and paste

Enjoy having their own books

Enjoy being read to if story is not too long

Enjoy rhythmical equipment: rocking chairs, swings

Play with dolls and stuffed animals

Play act: imaginary eating, sleeping

Begin to talk in short sentences

Often talk to themselves

Play individually with flexible scheduling

Begin to learn to use the toilet

Sit in a group for only a few minutes

Not adapt, give in, or be very patient

Not share toys or materials well

Not maintain attention span for more than a few minutes

MOST THREE YEAR OLDS CAN . . .

Walk quickly or run and walk a straight line

Climb stairs, jump off steps, and walk backwards

Ride a tricycle

Catch and throw a large ball without losing balance

Get undressed by themselves (not dressed)

Unbutton big buttons

Tear paper and paste in place

Exhibit high interest in water play

Make things from clay, mud, or sand

Begin painting with a brush on plain paper

Balance on toes or one foot for a short time

Look at picture books on their own

Name pictures of things in books

Begin to draw simple shapes

Build towers with blocks

Pour from a small pitcher

String large beads

Assemble large puzzle pieces

Put pegs in pegboard

Count two objects

Begin to learn to take turns, share, and listen to others

Play well next to others and make new friends

MOST FOUR YEAR OLDS CAN . . .

Love to run fast, skip, gallop, and climb

Love to talk and shout

Have a good sense of balance

Build complex structures and do stunts

Swing, whirl, and do somersaults

Walk up and down stairs, one foot to a step

Stand on one foot for up to 8 seconds

Begin to use roller skates

Ride a small bicycle with training wheels

Use hands to catch a smaller ball

Button, unbutton, and dress themselves

Lace shoes and string smaller beads

Cut on a line with scissors

Recognize and name basic colors

Carry a cup of water without spilling

Enjoy drawing, coloring, and painting

Put small groups of things in order

Match shapes and copy simple shapes

Follow dotted lines to link pictures

Cut a picture into pieces and put it back together

Begin to print letters, numbers, and their own first name

Learn more difficult speech sounds

Appreciate nature

Play imaginative games and pretend with dress up

Do puzzles and play dominoes and simple card games

Sing songs and tell stories

Recite rhymes and fingerplays

Beat out a rhythm well

Love being silly and making up words

Draw recognizable people

Brush teeth and take care of simple personal needs

Begin to play well with others

MOST FIVE YEAR OLDS CAN . . .

Hop, jump rope, and climb a jungle gym

Swim and/or ride a two wheel bike (some)

Enjoy building with both large and small blocks

Love to swing, skip, roller skate, jump from heights

Catch and throw fairly well

Love to play with simple materials and gadgets

Love being read to and looking at picture books

Love to sing and dance to records

Enjoy acting out with puppets

Name various body parts

Color within lines and copy things

Identify some small words

Recognize their own name

Say the alphabet and print some letters of the alphabet

Count up to twenty objects

Add and subtract correctly within five

Write numbers 1–10

Hammer a nail

Use scissors carefully

Learn by doing things themselves

Share more with others

Forget safety rules

Easily be distracted

Daily Lesson Plans

THEME: Bears

(Record your plans for group songs, stories, circle time, special events, outdoor activities, snacks, lunch, and naptime.)

TIMES and ACTIVITIES	MONDAY	TUESDAY	WEDNESDAY	THURSDAY	FRIDAY
8:30 Arrival Free Play	Stuffed bears	Direct children to table toys			
9:00 Circle Time Story Time	Hello Song Picture Book: "Goldilocks and the Three Bears" Jan Brett	Picture Book: "Bear Cubs" Anne Wendorff	Flannel Board: "Bear Wants More" Karma Wilson	Picture Book: "Bear Wants More" Karma Wilson	Rhyme: "This Little Bear" use stick puppets
9:30 Music Time Transition Time 10:00 Free Time	"Black Bear Song" Talk about how to be safe in the woods and around bears				
10:20 Wash Hands 10:30 Snack Clean-Up	Instant Oatmeal (honey, sugar, cups, hot water)	Apple pieces and juice	Bear Grahams and milk	blueberries and a cookie	Walking trip to park next to school. snack-trail mix
11:00 Center Time 11:45 Transition Time	Centers with a * on next page Shake rain stick - have children clap hands				
12:00 Wash hands 12:15 Lunch 12:45 Clean-up 1:00 Free play					
1:30 Circle Time Story Time 2:00 Nap Time	"Brown Bear, Brown Bear, What do you see?" Bill Martin, Jr.	"Now I Know Bears" Melvin and Gilda Berger	"Brown Bear"	"Now I Know Bears" Melvin and Gilda Berger	"Brown Bear"
		Have children bring teddy bears from home for nap time.			
3:00 Quiet Work Time 3:45 Clean-up 4:00 Dismissal	Centers with * on next page				

Weekly Activity/Interest Centers

(Record your ideas and planned seasonal/holiday changes for your classroom centers.)

ARTS AND CRAFTS	DRAMATIC PLAY	HOUSEKEEPING	BLOCKS AND BUILDING
Bear rubber stamps & ink pads *Bear masks (Paper plates, yarn, patterns, glue sticks)	Pretend to visit a bear cave. * Make a cave with blankets and chairs. Flashlights, backpacks	Set out play dishes and have children act out "Goldilocks and the Three Bears"	Build a bear cave with blocks.

OUTDOOR PLAY	LIBRARY/WRITING	MATH AND MANIPULATIVES	MUSIC AND MOVEMENT
Walk to park or playground. * Point out things that bears eat, colors of bears, etc. Talk about dangers of bears & woods	"My Book About Bears!" Make copies, kids color. Staple together to make booklets. *Scholastic Printables What do bears eat? Page 14 "Bear Cubs"	Sorting Bears (Muffin tin, counting bears) *Bear Puzzles Matching Number Bears	* Teddy Bear Song (kids act out movements) Bear: Thematic Song Scholastic Printables

COMPUTER	COOKING AND NUTRITION	TABLE TOYS	SAND AND WATER
Bubble Bear AlphaTales Interactive E-Storybook	Bear Trail Mix * (Sunflower seeds, raisins, chocolate chips, Cheerios®, mini marshmallows) small plastic bags Instant oatmeal for porridge	Bear Playset * Types of Bears matching cards	Hide plastic bear characters in the sand for children to find.

WEEK OF: _____ # Daily Lesson Plans **THEME:** _____

(Record your plans for group songs, stories, circle time, special events, outdoor activities, snacks, lunch, and naptime.)

TIMES and ACTIVITIES	MONDAY	TUESDAY	WEDNESDAY	THURSDAY	FRIDAY

Weekly Activity/Interest Centers

(Record your ideas and planned seasonal/holiday changes for your classroom centers.)

ARTS AND CRAFTS	DRAMATIC PLAY	HOUSEKEEPING	BLOCKS AND BUILDING

OUTDOOR PLAY	LIBRARY/WRITING	MATH AND MANIPULATIVES	MUSIC AND MOVEMENT

COMPUTER	COOKING AND NUTRITION	TABLE TOYS	SAND AND WATER

Daily Lesson Plans

WEEK OF: _____ THEME: _____

(Record your plans for group songs, stories, circle time, special events, outdoor activities, snacks, lunch, and naptime.)

TIMES and ACTIVITIES	MONDAY	TUESDAY	WEDNESDAY	THURSDAY	FRIDAY

Weekly Activity/Interest Centers

WEEK OF: _____

(Record your ideas and planned seasonal/holiday changes for your classroom centers.)

ARTS AND CRAFTS	DRAMATIC PLAY	HOUSEKEEPING	BLOCKS AND BUILDING

OUTDOOR PLAY	LIBRARY/WRITING	MATH AND MANIPULATIVES	MUSIC AND MOVEMENT

COMPUTER	COOKING AND NUTRITION	TABLE TOYS	SAND AND WATER

WEEK OF: _____  **THEME:** _____

(Record your plans for group songs, stories, circle time, special events, outdoor activities, snacks, lunch, and naptime.)

TIMES and ACTIVITIES	MONDAY	TUESDAY	WEDNESDAY	THURSDAY	FRIDAY

Weekly Activity/Interest Centers

WEEK OF:_____

(Record your ideas and planned seasonal/holiday changes for your classroom centers.)

ARTS AND CRAFTS	DRAMATIC PLAY	HOUSEKEEPING	BLOCKS AND BUILDING

OUTDOOR PLAY	LIBRARY/WRITING	MATH AND MANIPULATIVES	MUSIC AND MOVEMENT

COMPUTER	COOKING AND NUTRITION	TABLE TOYS	SAND AND WATER

Daily Lesson Plans

(Record your plans for group songs, stories, circle time, special events, outdoor activities, snacks, lunch, and naptime.)

TIMES and ACTIVITIES	MONDAY	TUESDAY	WEDNESDAY	THURSDAY	FRIDAY

Weekly Activity/Interest Centers

(Record your ideas and planned seasonal/holiday changes for your classroom centers.)

ARTS AND CRAFTS	DRAMATIC PLAY	HOUSEKEEPING	BLOCKS AND BUILDING

OUTDOOR PLAY	LIBRARY/WRITING	MATH AND MANIPULATIVES	MUSIC AND MOVEMENT

COMPUTER	COOKING AND NUTRITION	TABLE TOYS	SAND AND WATER

Daily Lesson Plans

(Record your plans for group songs, stories, circle time, special events, outdoor activities, snacks, lunch, and naptime.)

TIMES and ACTIVITIES	MONDAY	TUESDAY	WEDNESDAY	THURSDAY	FRIDAY

Weekly Activity/Interest Centers

(Record your ideas and planned seasonal/holiday changes for your classroom centers.)

ARTS AND CRAFTS	DRAMATIC PLAY	HOUSEKEEPING	BLOCKS AND BUILDING
OUTDOOR PLAY	**LIBRARY/WRITING**	**MATH AND MANIPULATIVES**	**MUSIC AND MOVEMENT**
COMPUTER	**COOKING AND NUTRITION**	**TABLE TOYS**	**SAND AND WATER**

WEEK OF: _____   THEME: _____

TIMES and ACTIVITIES	MONDAY	TUESDAY	WEDNESDAY	THURSDAY	FRIDAY
(Record your plans for group songs, stories, circle time, special events, outdoor activities, snacks, lunch, and naptime.)					

Weekly Activity/Interest Centers

WEEK OF:_____

(Record your ideas and planned seasonal/holiday changes for your classroom centers.)

ARTS AND CRAFTS	DRAMATIC PLAY	HOUSEKEEPING	BLOCKS AND BUILDING

OUTDOOR PLAY	LIBRARY/WRITING	MATH AND MANIPULATIVES	MUSIC AND MOVEMENT

COMPUTER	COOKING AND NUTRITION	TABLE TOYS	SAND AND WATER

Daily Lesson Plans

(Record your plans for group songs, stories, circle time, special events, outdoor activities, snacks, lunch, and naptime.)

TIMES and ACTIVITIES	MONDAY	TUESDAY	WEDNESDAY	THURSDAY	FRIDAY

Weekly Activity/Interest Centers

WEEK OF:_____

(Record your ideas and planned seasonal/holiday changes for your classroom centers.)

ARTS AND CRAFTS	DRAMATIC PLAY	HOUSEKEEPING	BLOCKS AND BUILDING

OUTDOOR PLAY	LIBRARY/WRITING	MATH AND MANIPULATIVES	MUSIC AND MOVEMENT

COMPUTER	COOKING AND NUTRITION	TABLE TOYS	SAND AND WATER

(Record your plans for group songs, stories, circle time, special events, outdoor activities, snacks, lunch, and naptime.)

TIMES and ACTIVITIES	MONDAY	TUESDAY	WEDNESDAY	THURSDAY	FRIDAY

Weekly Activity/Interest Centers

WEEK OF:_____

(Record your ideas and planned seasonal/holiday changes for your classroom centers.)

ARTS AND CRAFTS	DRAMATIC PLAY	HOUSEKEEPING	BLOCKS AND BUILDING

OUTDOOR PLAY	LIBRARY/WRITING	MATH AND MANIPULATIVES	MUSIC AND MOVEMENT

COMPUTER	COOKING AND NUTRITION	TABLE TOYS	SAND AND WATER

WEEK OF:_____ ## Daily Lesson Plans THEME:_____

(Record your plans for group songs, stories, circle time, special events, outdoor activities, snacks, lunch, and naptime.)

TIMES and ACTIVITIES	MONDAY	TUESDAY	WEDNESDAY	THURSDAY	FRIDAY

Weekly Activity/Interest Centers

WEEK OF:_____

(Record your ideas and planned seasonal/holiday changes for your classroom centers.)

ARTS AND CRAFTS	DRAMATIC PLAY	HOUSEKEEPING	BLOCKS AND BUILDING
OUTDOOR PLAY	**LIBRARY/WRITING**	**MATH AND MANIPULATIVES**	**MUSIC AND MOVEMENT**
COMPUTER	**COOKING AND NUTRITION**	**TABLE TOYS**	**SAND AND WATER**

Daily Lesson Plans

WEEK OF:_____ THEME:_____

(Record your plans for group songs, stories, circle time, special events, outdoor activities, snacks, lunch, and naptime.)

TIMES and ACTIVITIES	MONDAY	TUESDAY	WEDNESDAY	THURSDAY	FRIDAY

Weekly Activity/Interest Centers

(Record your ideas and planned seasonal/holiday changes for your classroom centers.)

ARTS AND CRAFTS	DRAMATIC PLAY	HOUSEKEEPING	BLOCKS AND BUILDING

OUTDOOR PLAY	LIBRARY/WRITING	MATH AND MANIPULATIVES	MUSIC AND MOVEMENT

COMPUTER	COOKING AND NUTRITION	TABLE TOYS	SAND AND WATER

Daily Lesson Plans

(Record your plans for group songs, stories, circle time, special events, outdoor activities, snacks, lunch, and naptime.)

TIMES and ACTIVITIES	MONDAY	TUESDAY	WEDNESDAY	THURSDAY	FRIDAY

Weekly Activity/Interest Centers

WEEK OF: _____

(Record your ideas and planned seasonal/holiday changes for your classroom centers.)

ARTS AND CRAFTS	DRAMATIC PLAY	HOUSEKEEPING	BLOCKS AND BUILDING
OUTDOOR PLAY	**LIBRARY/WRITING**	**MATH AND MANIPULATIVES**	**MUSIC AND MOVEMENT**
COMPUTER	**COOKING AND NUTRITION**	**TABLE TOYS**	**SAND AND WATER**

Daily Lesson Plans

THEME: _____

(Record your plans for group songs, stories, circle time, special events, outdoor activities, snacks, lunch, and naptime.)

TIMES and ACTIVITIES	MONDAY	TUESDAY	WEDNESDAY	THURSDAY	FRIDAY

Weekly Activity/Interest Centers

WEEK OF:_____

(Record your ideas and planned seasonal/holiday changes for your classroom centers.)

ARTS AND CRAFTS	DRAMATIC PLAY	HOUSEKEEPING	BLOCKS AND BUILDING
OUTDOOR PLAY	**LIBRARY/WRITING**	**MATH AND MANIPULATIVES**	**MUSIC AND MOVEMENT**
COMPUTER	**COOKING AND NUTRITION**	**TABLE TOYS**	**SAND AND WATER**

Daily Lesson Plans

THEME: _____

(Record your plans for group songs, stories, circle time, special events, outdoor activities, snacks, lunch, and naptime.)

TIMES and ACTIVITIES	MONDAY	TUESDAY	WEDNESDAY	THURSDAY	FRIDAY

Weekly Activity/Interest Centers

WEEK OF:_____

(Record your ideas and planned seasonal/holiday changes for your classroom centers.)

ARTS AND CRAFTS	DRAMATIC PLAY	HOUSEKEEPING	BLOCKS AND BUILDING

OUTDOOR PLAY	LIBRARY/WRITING	MATH AND MANIPULATIVES	MUSIC AND MOVEMENT

COMPUTER	COOKING AND NUTRITION	TABLE TOYS	SAND AND WATER

Daily Lesson Plans

WEEK OF:_____

THEME:_____

(Record your plans for group songs, stories, circle time, special events, outdoor activities, snacks, lunch, and naptime.)

TIMES and ACTIVITIES	MONDAY	TUESDAY	WEDNESDAY	THURSDAY	FRIDAY

Weekly Activity/Interest Centers

(Record your ideas and planned seasonal/holiday changes for your classroom centers.)

ARTS AND CRAFTS	DRAMATIC PLAY	HOUSEKEEPING	BLOCKS AND BUILDING
OUTDOOR PLAY	**LIBRARY/WRITING**	**MATH AND MANIPULATIVES**	**MUSIC AND MOVEMENT**
COMPUTER	**COOKING AND NUTRITION**	**TABLE TOYS**	**SAND AND WATER**

Daily Lesson Plans

WEEK OF:_____ THEME:_____

(Record your plans for group songs, stories, circle time, special events, outdoor activities, snacks, lunch, and naptime.)

TIMES and ACTIVITIES	MONDAY	TUESDAY	WEDNESDAY	THURSDAY	FRIDAY

Weekly Activity/Interest Centers

(Record your ideas and planned seasonal/holiday changes for your classroom centers.)

ARTS AND CRAFTS	DRAMATIC PLAY	HOUSEKEEPING	BLOCKS AND BUILDING

OUTDOOR PLAY	LIBRARY/WRITING	MATH AND MANIPULATIVES	MUSIC AND MOVEMENT

COMPUTER	COOKING AND NUTRITION	TABLE TOYS	SAND AND WATER

Daily Lesson Plans

WEEK OF: _____   THEME: _____

(Record your plans for group songs, stories, circle time, special events, outdoor activities, snacks, lunch, and naptime.)

TIMES and ACTIVITIES	MONDAY	TUESDAY	WEDNESDAY	THURSDAY	FRIDAY

Weekly Activity/Interest Centers

WEEK OF:_____

(Record your ideas and planned seasonal/holiday changes for your classroom centers.)

ARTS AND CRAFTS	DRAMATIC PLAY	HOUSEKEEPING	BLOCKS AND BUILDING

OUTDOOR PLAY	LIBRARY/WRITING	MATH AND MANIPULATIVES	MUSIC AND MOVEMENT

COMPUTER	COOKING AND NUTRITION	TABLE TOYS	SAND AND WATER

WEEK OF:_____ **Daily Lesson Plans** THEME:_____

(Record your plans for group songs, stories, circle time, special events, outdoor activities, snacks, lunch, and naptime.)

TIMES and ACTIVITIES	MONDAY	TUESDAY	WEDNESDAY	THURSDAY	FRIDAY

Weekly Activity/Interest Centers

(Record your ideas and planned seasonal/holiday changes for your classroom centers.)

ARTS AND CRAFTS	DRAMATIC PLAY	HOUSEKEEPING	BLOCKS AND BUILDING

OUTDOOR PLAY	LIBRARY/WRITING	MATH AND MANIPULATIVES	MUSIC AND MOVEMENT

COMPUTER	COOKING AND NUTRITION	TABLE TOYS	SAND AND WATER

Daily Lesson Plans

(Record your plans for group songs, stories, circle time, special events, outdoor activities, snacks, lunch, and naptime.)

TIMES and ACTIVITIES	MONDAY	TUESDAY	WEDNESDAY	THURSDAY	FRIDAY

Weekly Activity/Interest Centers

WEEK OF:_____

(Record your ideas and planned seasonal/holiday changes for your classroom centers.)

ARTS AND CRAFTS	DRAMATIC PLAY	HOUSEKEEPING	BLOCKS AND BUILDING

OUTDOOR PLAY	LIBRARY/WRITING	MATH AND MANIPULATIVES	MUSIC AND MOVEMENT

COMPUTER	COOKING AND NUTRITION	TABLE TOYS	SAND AND WATER

© Scholastic Inc.

Daily Lesson Plans

(Record your plans for group songs, stories, circle time, special events, outdoor activities, snacks, lunch, and naptime.)

TIMES and ACTIVITIES	MONDAY	TUESDAY	WEDNESDAY	THURSDAY	FRIDAY

Weekly Activity/Interest Centers

WEEK OF:_____

(Record your ideas and planned seasonal/holiday changes for your classroom centers.)

ARTS AND CRAFTS	DRAMATIC PLAY	HOUSEKEEPING	BLOCKS AND BUILDING

OUTDOOR PLAY	LIBRARY/WRITING	MATH AND MANIPULATIVES	MUSIC AND MOVEMENT

COMPUTER	COOKING AND NUTRITION	TABLE TOYS	SAND AND WATER

Daily Lesson Plans

WEEK OF: _____

THEME: _____

(Record your plans for group songs, stories, circle time, special events, outdoor activities, snacks, lunch, and naptime.)

TIMES and ACTIVITIES	MONDAY	TUESDAY	WEDNESDAY	THURSDAY	FRIDAY

Weekly Activity/Interest Centers

WEEK OF:_____

(Record your ideas and planned seasonal/holiday changes for your classroom centers.)

ARTS AND CRAFTS	DRAMATIC PLAY	HOUSEKEEPING	BLOCKS AND BUILDING

OUTDOOR PLAY	LIBRARY/WRITING	MATH AND MANIPULATIVES	MUSIC AND MOVEMENT

COMPUTER	COOKING AND NUTRITION	TABLE TOYS	SAND AND WATER

55

Daily Lesson Plans

WEEK OF: _____ THEME: _____

(Record your plans for group songs, stories, circle time, special events, outdoor activities, snacks, lunch, and naptime.)

TIMES and ACTIVITIES	MONDAY	TUESDAY	WEDNESDAY	THURSDAY	FRIDAY

Weekly Activity/Interest Centers

WEEK OF:_____

(Record your ideas and planned seasonal/holiday changes for your classroom centers.)

ARTS AND CRAFTS	DRAMATIC PLAY	HOUSEKEEPING	BLOCKS AND BUILDING

OUTDOOR PLAY	LIBRARY/WRITING	MATH AND MANIPULATIVES	MUSIC AND MOVEMENT

COMPUTER	COOKING AND NUTRITION	TABLE TOYS	SAND AND WATER

Daily Lesson Plans

(Record your plans for group songs, stories, circle time, special events, outdoor activities, snacks, lunch, and naptime.)

TIMES and ACTIVITIES	MONDAY	TUESDAY	WEDNESDAY	THURSDAY	FRIDAY

Weekly Activity/Interest Centers

WEEK OF:_____

(Record your ideas and planned seasonal/holiday changes for your classroom centers.)

ARTS AND CRAFTS	DRAMATIC PLAY	HOUSEKEEPING	BLOCKS AND BUILDING
OUTDOOR PLAY	**LIBRARY/WRITING**	**MATH AND MANIPULATIVES**	**MUSIC AND MOVEMENT**
COMPUTER	**COOKING AND NUTRITION**	**TABLE TOYS**	**SAND AND WATER**

WEEK OF: _____ **THEME:** _____

(Record your plans for group songs, stories, circle time, special events, outdoor activities, snacks, lunch, and naptime.)

TIMES and ACTIVITIES	MONDAY	TUESDAY	WEDNESDAY	THURSDAY	FRIDAY

Weekly Activity/Interest Centers

(Record your ideas and planned seasonal/holiday changes for your classroom centers.)

ARTS AND CRAFTS	DRAMATIC PLAY	HOUSEKEEPING	BLOCKS AND BUILDING

OUTDOOR PLAY	LIBRARY/WRITING	MATH AND MANIPULATIVES	MUSIC AND MOVEMENT

COMPUTER	COOKING AND NUTRITION	TABLE TOYS	SAND AND WATER

Daily Lesson Plans

(Record your plans for group songs, stories, circle time, special events, outdoor activities, snacks, lunch, and naptime.)

TIMES and ACTIVITIES	MONDAY	TUESDAY	WEDNESDAY	THURSDAY	FRIDAY

Weekly Activity/Interest Centers

WEEK OF:_____

(Record your ideas and planned seasonal/holiday changes for your classroom centers.)

ARTS AND CRAFTS	DRAMATIC PLAY	HOUSEKEEPING	BLOCKS AND BUILDING

OUTDOOR PLAY	LIBRARY/WRITING	MATH AND MANIPULATIVES	MUSIC AND MOVEMENT

COMPUTER	COOKING AND NUTRITION	TABLE TOYS	SAND AND WATER

Daily Lesson Plans

WEEK OF:_____   THEME:_____

(Record your plans for group songs, stories, circle time, special events, outdoor activities, snacks, lunch, and naptime.)

TIMES and ACTIVITIES	MONDAY	TUESDAY	WEDNESDAY	THURSDAY	FRIDAY

Weekly Activity/Interest Centers

WEEK OF:_____

(Record your ideas and planned seasonal/holiday changes for your classroom centers.)

ARTS AND CRAFTS	DRAMATIC PLAY	HOUSEKEEPING	BLOCKS AND BUILDING

OUTDOOR PLAY	LIBRARY/WRITING	MATH AND MANIPULATIVES	MUSIC AND MOVEMENT

COMPUTER	COOKING AND NUTRITION	TABLE TOYS	SAND AND WATER

Daily Lesson Plans

(Record your plans for group songs, stories, circle time, special events, outdoor activities, snacks, lunch, and naptime.)

TIMES and ACTIVITIES	MONDAY	TUESDAY	WEDNESDAY	THURSDAY	FRIDAY

Weekly Activity/Interest Centers

WEEK OF:_____

(Record your ideas and planned seasonal/holiday changes for your classroom centers.)

ARTS AND CRAFTS	DRAMATIC PLAY	HOUSEKEEPING	BLOCKS AND BUILDING

OUTDOOR PLAY	LIBRARY/WRITING	MATH AND MANIPULATIVES	MUSIC AND MOVEMENT

COMPUTER	COOKING AND NUTRITION	TABLE TOYS	SAND AND WATER

Daily Lesson Plans

WEEK OF:_____ THEME:_____

(Record your plans for group songs, stories, circle time, special events, outdoor activities, snacks, lunch, and naptime.)

TIMES and ACTIVITIES	MONDAY	TUESDAY	WEDNESDAY	THURSDAY	FRIDAY

Weekly Activity/Interest Centers

WEEK OF: _____

(Record your ideas and planned seasonal/holiday changes for your classroom centers.)

ARTS AND CRAFTS	DRAMATIC PLAY	HOUSEKEEPING	BLOCKS AND BUILDING

OUTDOOR PLAY	LIBRARY/WRITING	MATH AND MANIPULATIVES	MUSIC AND MOVEMENT

COMPUTER	COOKING AND NUTRITION	TABLE TOYS	SAND AND WATER

WEEK OF:_____ # Daily Lesson Plans THEME:_____

(Record your plans for group songs, stories, circle time, special events, outdoor activities, snacks, lunch, and naptime.)

TIMES and ACTIVITIES	MONDAY	TUESDAY	WEDNESDAY	THURSDAY	FRIDAY

Weekly Activity/Interest Centers

WEEK OF:_____

(Record your ideas and planned seasonal/holiday changes for your classroom centers.)

ARTS AND CRAFTS	DRAMATIC PLAY	HOUSEKEEPING	BLOCKS AND BUILDING
OUTDOOR PLAY	**LIBRARY/WRITING**	**MATH AND MANIPULATIVES**	**MUSIC AND MOVEMENT**
COMPUTER	**COOKING AND NUTRITION**	**TABLE TOYS**	**SAND AND WATER**

(Record your plans for group songs, stories, circle time, special events, outdoor activities, snacks, lunch, and naptime.)

TIMES and ACTIVITIES	MONDAY	TUESDAY	WEDNESDAY	THURSDAY	FRIDAY

Weekly Activity/Interest Centers

WEEK OF: _____

(Record your ideas and planned seasonal/holiday changes for your classroom centers.)

ARTS AND CRAFTS	DRAMATIC PLAY	HOUSEKEEPING	BLOCKS AND BUILDING

OUTDOOR PLAY	LIBRARY/WRITING	MATH AND MANIPULATIVES	MUSIC AND MOVEMENT

COMPUTER	COOKING AND NUTRITION	TABLE TOYS	SAND AND WATER

Daily Lesson Plans

(Record your plans for group songs, stories, circle time, special events, outdoor activities, snacks, lunch, and naptime.)

TIMES and ACTIVITIES	MONDAY	TUESDAY	WEDNESDAY	THURSDAY	FRIDAY

Weekly Activity/Interest Centers

WEEK OF: _____

(Record your ideas and planned seasonal/holiday changes for your classroom centers.)

ARTS AND CRAFTS	DRAMATIC PLAY	HOUSEKEEPING	BLOCKS AND BUILDING

OUTDOOR PLAY	LIBRARY/WRITING	MATH AND MANIPULATIVES	MUSIC AND MOVEMENT

COMPUTER	COOKING AND NUTRITION	TABLE TOYS	SAND AND WATER

WEEK OF: _____  **THEME:** _____

(Record your plans for group songs, stories, circle time, special events, outdoor activities, snacks, lunch, and naptime.)

TIMES and ACTIVITIES	MONDAY	TUESDAY	WEDNESDAY	THURSDAY	FRIDAY

Weekly Activity/Interest Centers

WEEK OF:_____

(Record your ideas and planned seasonal/holiday changes for your classroom centers.)

ARTS AND CRAFTS	DRAMATIC PLAY	HOUSEKEEPING	BLOCKS AND BUILDING

OUTDOOR PLAY	LIBRARY/WRITING	MATH AND MANIPULATIVES	MUSIC AND MOVEMENT

COMPUTER	COOKING AND NUTRITION	TABLE TOYS	SAND AND WATER

Daily Lesson Plans

WEEK OF:_____   THEME:_____

(Record your plans for group songs, stories, circle time, special events, outdoor activities, snacks, lunch, and naptime.)

TIMES and ACTIVITIES	MONDAY	TUESDAY	WEDNESDAY	THURSDAY	FRIDAY

78

© Scholastic Inc.

Weekly Activity/Interest Centers

WEEK OF: _____

(Record your ideas and planned seasonal/holiday changes for your classroom centers.)

ARTS AND CRAFTS	DRAMATIC PLAY	HOUSEKEEPING	BLOCKS AND BUILDING

OUTDOOR PLAY	LIBRARY/WRITING	MATH AND MANIPULATIVES	MUSIC AND MOVEMENT

COMPUTER	COOKING AND NUTRITION	TABLE TOYS	SAND AND WATER

WEEK OF: _____  **THEME:** _____

(Record your plans for group songs, stories, circle time, special events, outdoor activities, snacks, lunch, and naptime.)

TIMES and ACTIVITIES	MONDAY	TUESDAY	WEDNESDAY	THURSDAY	FRIDAY

Weekly Activity/Interest Centers

WEEK OF: _____

(Record your ideas and planned seasonal/holiday changes for your classroom centers.)

ARTS AND CRAFTS	DRAMATIC PLAY	HOUSEKEEPING	BLOCKS AND BUILDING

OUTDOOR PLAY	LIBRARY/WRITING	MATH AND MANIPULATIVES	MUSIC AND MOVEMENT

COMPUTER	COOKING AND NUTRITION	TABLE TOYS	SAND AND WATER

Daily Lesson Plans

WEEK OF: _____ **THEME:** _____

(Record your plans for group songs, stories, circle time, special events, outdoor activities, snacks, lunch, and naptime.)

TIMES and ACTIVITIES	MONDAY	TUESDAY	WEDNESDAY	THURSDAY	FRIDAY

Weekly Activity/Interest Centers

(Record your ideas and planned seasonal/holiday changes for your classroom centers.)

ARTS AND CRAFTS	DRAMATIC PLAY	HOUSEKEEPING	BLOCKS AND BUILDING

OUTDOOR PLAY	LIBRARY/WRITING	MATH AND MANIPULATIVES	MUSIC AND MOVEMENT

COMPUTER	COOKING AND NUTRITION	TABLE TOYS	SAND AND WATER

Daily Lesson Plans

WEEK OF:_____   THEME:_____

(Record your plans for group songs, stories, circle time, special events, outdoor activities, snacks, lunch, and naptime.)

TIMES and ACTIVITIES	MONDAY	TUESDAY	WEDNESDAY	THURSDAY	FRIDAY

Weekly Activity/Interest Centers

WEEK OF:_____

(Record your ideas and planned seasonal/holiday changes for your classroom centers.)

ARTS AND CRAFTS	DRAMATIC PLAY	HOUSEKEEPING	BLOCKS AND BUILDING

OUTDOOR PLAY	LIBRARY/WRITING	MATH AND MANIPULATIVES	MUSIC AND MOVEMENT

COMPUTER	COOKING AND NUTRITION	TABLE TOYS	SAND AND WATER

Daily Lesson Plans

(Record your plans for group songs, stories, circle time, special events, outdoor activities, snacks, lunch, and naptime.)

TIMES and ACTIVITIES	MONDAY	TUESDAY	WEDNESDAY	THURSDAY	FRIDAY

Weekly Activity/Interest Centers

(Record your ideas and planned seasonal/holiday changes for your classroom centers.)

ARTS AND CRAFTS	DRAMATIC PLAY	HOUSEKEEPING	BLOCKS AND BUILDING

OUTDOOR PLAY	LIBRARY/WRITING	MATH AND MANIPULATIVES	MUSIC AND MOVEMENT

COMPUTER	COOKING AND NUTRITION	TABLE TOYS	SAND AND WATER

Daily Lesson Plans

WEEK OF:_____ **THEME:** _____

(Record your plans for group songs, stories, circle time, special events, outdoor activities, snacks, lunch, and naptime.)

TIMES and ACTIVITIES	MONDAY	TUESDAY	WEDNESDAY	THURSDAY	FRIDAY

Weekly Activity/Interest Centers

WEEK OF:_____

(Record your ideas and planned seasonal/holiday changes for your classroom centers.)

ARTS AND CRAFTS	DRAMATIC PLAY	HOUSEKEEPING	BLOCKS AND BUILDING

OUTDOOR PLAY	LIBRARY/WRITING	MATH AND MANIPULATIVES	MUSIC AND MOVEMENT

COMPUTER	COOKING AND NUTRITION	TABLE TOYS	SAND AND WATER

Daily Lesson Plans

WEEK OF:_____   **THEME:**_____

(Record your plans for group songs, stories, circle time, special events, outdoor activities, snacks, lunch, and naptime.)

TIMES and ACTIVITIES	MONDAY	TUESDAY	WEDNESDAY	THURSDAY	FRIDAY

Weekly Activity/Interest Centers

WEEK OF:_____

(Record your ideas and planned seasonal/holiday changes for your classroom centers.)

ARTS AND CRAFTS	DRAMATIC PLAY	HOUSEKEEPING	BLOCKS AND BUILDING

OUTDOOR PLAY	LIBRARY/WRITING	MATH AND MANIPULATIVES	MUSIC AND MOVEMENT

COMPUTER	COOKING AND NUTRITION	TABLE TOYS	SAND AND WATER

Daily Lesson Plans

(Record your plans for group songs, stories, circle time, special events, outdoor activities, snacks, lunch, and naptime.)

TIMES and ACTIVITIES	MONDAY	TUESDAY	WEDNESDAY	THURSDAY	FRIDAY

Weekly Activity/Interest Centers

WEEK OF:_____

(Record your ideas and planned seasonal/holiday changes for your classroom centers.)

ARTS AND CRAFTS	DRAMATIC PLAY	HOUSEKEEPING	BLOCKS AND BUILDING

OUTDOOR PLAY	LIBRARY/WRITING	MATH AND MANIPULATIVES	MUSIC AND MOVEMENT

COMPUTER	COOKING AND NUTRITION	TABLE TOYS	SAND AND WATER

Daily Lesson Plans

(Record your plans for group songs, stories, circle time, special events, outdoor activities, snacks, lunch, and naptime.)

TIMES and ACTIVITIES	MONDAY	TUESDAY	WEDNESDAY	THURSDAY	FRIDAY

Weekly Activity/Interest Centers

WEEK OF:_____

(Record your ideas and planned seasonal/holiday changes for your classroom centers.)

ARTS AND CRAFTS	DRAMATIC PLAY	HOUSEKEEPING	BLOCKS AND BUILDING
OUTDOOR PLAY	**LIBRARY/WRITING**	**MATH AND MANIPULATIVES**	**MUSIC AND MOVEMENT**
COMPUTER	**COOKING AND NUTRITION**	**TABLE TOYS**	**SAND AND WATER**

© Scholastic Inc.

Daily Lesson Plans

(Record your plans for group songs, stories, circle time, special events, outdoor activities, snacks, lunch, and naptime.)

TIMES and ACTIVITIES	MONDAY	TUESDAY	WEDNESDAY	THURSDAY	FRIDAY

Weekly Activity/Interest Centers

WEEK OF: _____

(Record your ideas and planned seasonal/holiday changes for your classroom centers.)

ARTS AND CRAFTS	DRAMATIC PLAY	HOUSEKEEPING	BLOCKS AND BUILDING
OUTDOOR PLAY	**LIBRARY/WRITING**	**MATH AND MANIPULATIVES**	**MUSIC AND MOVEMENT**
COMPUTER	**COOKING AND NUTRITION**	**TABLE TOYS**	**SAND AND WATER**

Daily Lesson Plans

WEEK OF: _____ **THEME:** _____

(Record your plans for group songs, stories, circle time, special events, outdoor activities, snacks, lunch, and naptime.)

TIMES and ACTIVITIES	MONDAY	TUESDAY	WEDNESDAY	THURSDAY	FRIDAY

Weekly Activity/Interest Centers

WEEK OF:_____

(Record your ideas and planned seasonal/holiday changes for your classroom centers.)

ARTS AND CRAFTS	DRAMATIC PLAY	HOUSEKEEPING	BLOCKS AND BUILDING

OUTDOOR PLAY	LIBRARY/WRITING	MATH AND MANIPULATIVES	MUSIC AND MOVEMENT

COMPUTER	COOKING AND NUTRITION	TABLE TOYS	SAND AND WATER

Daily Lesson Plans

WEEK OF: _____   **THEME:** _____

(Record your plans for group songs, stories, circle time, special events, outdoor activities, snacks, lunch, and naptime.)

TIMES and ACTIVITIES	MONDAY	TUESDAY	WEDNESDAY	THURSDAY	FRIDAY

Weekly Activity/Interest Centers

WEEK OF:_____

(Record your ideas and planned seasonal/holiday changes for your classroom centers.)

ARTS AND CRAFTS	DRAMATIC PLAY	HOUSEKEEPING	BLOCKS AND BUILDING

OUTDOOR PLAY	LIBRARY/WRITING	MATH AND MANIPULATIVES	MUSIC AND MOVEMENT

COMPUTER	COOKING AND NUTRITION	TABLE TOYS	SAND AND WATER

Daily Lesson Plans

WEEK OF:_____

THEME:_____

(Record your plans for group songs, stories, circle time, special events, outdoor activities, snacks, lunch, and naptime.)

TIMES and ACTIVITIES	MONDAY	TUESDAY	WEDNESDAY	THURSDAY	FRIDAY

Weekly Activity/Interest Centers

(Record your ideas and planned seasonal/holiday changes for your classroom centers.)

ARTS AND CRAFTS	DRAMATIC PLAY	HOUSEKEEPING	BLOCKS AND BUILDING

OUTDOOR PLAY	LIBRARY/WRITING	MATH AND MANIPULATIVES	MUSIC AND MOVEMENT

COMPUTER	COOKING AND NUTRITION	TABLE TOYS	SAND AND WATER

Daily Lesson Plans

(Record your plans for group songs, stories, circle time, special events, outdoor activities, snacks, lunch, and naptime.)

TIMES and ACTIVITIES	MONDAY	TUESDAY	WEDNESDAY	THURSDAY	FRIDAY

Weekly Activity/Interest Centers

WEEK OF:_____

(Record your ideas and planned seasonal/holiday changes for your classroom centers.)

ARTS AND CRAFTS	DRAMATIC PLAY	HOUSEKEEPING	BLOCKS AND BUILDING

OUTDOOR PLAY	LIBRARY/WRITING	MATH AND MANIPULATIVES	MUSIC AND MOVEMENT

COMPUTER	COOKING AND NUTRITION	TABLE TOYS	SAND AND WATER

Daily Lesson Plans

(Record your plans for group songs, stories, circle time, special events, outdoor activities, snacks, lunch, and naptime.)

TIMES and ACTIVITIES	MONDAY	TUESDAY	WEDNESDAY	THURSDAY	FRIDAY

Weekly Activity/Interest Centers

WEEK OF:_____

(Record your ideas and planned seasonal/holiday changes for your classroom centers.)

ARTS AND CRAFTS	DRAMATIC PLAY	HOUSEKEEPING	BLOCKS AND BUILDING

OUTDOOR PLAY	LIBRARY/WRITING	MATH AND MANIPULATIVES	MUSIC AND MOVEMENT

COMPUTER	COOKING AND NUTRITION	TABLE TOYS	SAND AND WATER

Daily Lesson Plans

WEEK OF: _____   **THEME:** _____

(Record your plans for group songs, stories, circle time, special events, outdoor activities, snacks, lunch, and naptime.)

TIMES and ACTIVITIES	MONDAY	TUESDAY	WEDNESDAY	THURSDAY	FRIDAY

Weekly Activity/Interest Centers

WEEK OF: _____

(Record your ideas and planned seasonal/holiday changes for your classroom centers.)

ARTS AND CRAFTS	DRAMATIC PLAY	HOUSEKEEPING	BLOCKS AND BUILDING

OUTDOOR PLAY	LIBRARY/WRITING	MATH AND MANIPULATIVES	MUSIC AND MOVEMENT

COMPUTER	COOKING AND NUTRITION	TABLE TOYS	SAND AND WATER

Daily Lesson Plans

(Record your plans for group songs, stories, circle time, special events, outdoor activities, snacks, lunch, and naptime.)

TIMES and ACTIVITIES	MONDAY	TUESDAY	WEDNESDAY	THURSDAY	FRIDAY

Weekly Activity/Interest Centers

WEEK OF:_____

(Record your ideas and planned seasonal/holiday changes for your classroom centers.)

ARTS AND CRAFTS	DRAMATIC PLAY	HOUSEKEEPING	BLOCKS AND BUILDING

OUTDOOR PLAY	LIBRARY/WRITING	MATH AND MANIPULATIVES	MUSIC AND MOVEMENT

COMPUTER	COOKING AND NUTRITION	TABLE TOYS	SAND AND WATER

Daily Lesson Plans

(Record your plans for group songs, stories, circle time, special events, outdoor activities, snacks, lunch, and naptime.)

TIMES and ACTIVITIES	MONDAY	TUESDAY	WEDNESDAY	THURSDAY	FRIDAY

Weekly Activity/Interest Centers

WEEK OF:_____

(Record your ideas and planned seasonal/holiday changes for your classroom centers.)

ARTS AND CRAFTS	DRAMATIC PLAY	HOUSEKEEPING	BLOCKS AND BUILDING

OUTDOOR PLAY	LIBRARY/WRITING	MATH AND MANIPULATIVES	MUSIC AND MOVEMENT

COMPUTER	COOKING AND NUTRITION	TABLE TOYS	SAND AND WATER

Daily Lesson Plans

(Record your plans for group songs, stories, circle time, special events, outdoor activities, snacks, lunch, and naptime.)

TIMES and ACTIVITIES	MONDAY	TUESDAY	WEDNESDAY	THURSDAY	FRIDAY

Weekly Activity/Interest Centers

WEEK OF:_____

(Record your ideas and planned seasonal/holiday changes for your classroom centers.)

ARTS AND CRAFTS	DRAMATIC PLAY	HOUSEKEEPING	BLOCKS AND BUILDING

OUTDOOR PLAY	LIBRARY/WRITING	MATH AND MANIPULATIVES	MUSIC AND MOVEMENT

COMPUTER	COOKING AND NUTRITION	TABLE TOYS	SAND AND WATER

Daily Lesson Plans

(Record your plans for group songs, stories, circle time, special events, outdoor activities, snacks, lunch, and naptime.)

TIMES and ACTIVITIES	MONDAY	TUESDAY	WEDNESDAY	THURSDAY	FRIDAY

Weekly Activity/Interest Centers

WEEK OF:_____

(Record your ideas and planned seasonal/holiday changes for your classroom centers.)

ARTS AND CRAFTS	DRAMATIC PLAY	HOUSEKEEPING	BLOCKS AND BUILDING
OUTDOOR PLAY	**LIBRARY/WRITING**	**MATH AND MANIPULATIVES**	**MUSIC AND MOVEMENT**
COMPUTER	**COOKING AND NUTRITION**	**TABLE TOYS**	**SAND AND WATER**

Parent-Teacher Communications Log

Date: _____ Phone Letter Note Visit	Student: _____ Parent/ Guardian: _____ Reason: _____ _____	Notes:
Date: _____ Phone Letter Note Visit	Student: _____ Parent/ Guardian: _____ Reason: _____ _____	Notes:
Date: _____ Phone Letter Note Visit	Student: _____ Parent/ Guardian: _____ Reason: _____ _____	Notes:
Date: _____ Phone Letter Note Visit	Student: _____ Parent/ Guardian: _____ Reason: _____ _____	Notes:
Date: _____ Phone Letter Note Visit	Student: _____ Parent/ Guardian: _____ Reason: _____ _____	Notes:
Date: _____ Phone Letter Note Visit	Student: _____ Parent/ Guardian: _____ Reason: _____ _____	Notes:

☆ Parent-Teacher Communications Log

| Date: _____ | Student: _____ | Notes: |
| Phone   Letter

Note   Visit | Parent/
Guardian: _____
Reason: _____
_____ | |

| Date: _____ | Student: _____ | Notes: |
| Phone   Letter

Note   Visit | Parent/
Guardian: _____
Reason: _____
_____ | |

| Date: _____ | Student: _____ | Notes: |
| Phone   Letter

Note   Visit | Parent/
Guardian: _____
Reason: _____
_____ | |

| Date: _____ | Student: _____ | Notes: |
| Phone   Letter

Note   Visit | Parent/
Guardian: _____
Reason: _____
_____ | |

| Date: _____ | Student: _____ | Notes: |
| Phone   Letter

Note   Visit | Parent/
Guardian: _____
Reason: _____
_____ | |

| Date: _____ | Student: _____ | Notes: |
| Phone   Letter

Note   Visit | Parent/
Guardian: _____
Reason: _____
_____ | |

☆ Personal Telephone/Addresses

Name: _____
Address: _____
Phone: _____
E-Mail: _____

Name: _____
Address: _____
Phone: _____
E-Mail: _____

Name: _____
Address: _____
Phone: _____
E-Mail: _____

Name: _____
Address: _____
Phone: _____
E-Mail: _____

Name: _____
Address: _____
Phone: _____
E-Mail: _____

Name: _____
Address: _____
Phone: _____
E-Mail: _____

Name: _____
Address: _____
Phone: _____
E-Mail: _____

Name: _____
Address: _____
Phone: _____
E-Mail: _____

Name: _____
Address: _____
Phone: _____
E-Mail: _____

Name: _____
Address: _____
Phone: _____
E-Mail: _____

Name: _____
Address: _____
Phone: _____
E-Mail: _____

Name: _____
Address: _____
Phone: _____
E-Mail: _____

Name: _____
Address: _____
Phone: _____
E-Mail: _____

Name: _____
Address: _____
Phone: _____
E-Mail: _____

Name: _____
Address: _____
Phone: _____
E-Mail: _____

Name: _____
Address: _____
Phone: _____
E-Mail: _____

Name: _____
Address: _____
Phone: _____
E Mail: _____

Name: _____
Address: _____
Phone: _____
E-Mail: _____